A HANDBOOK OF
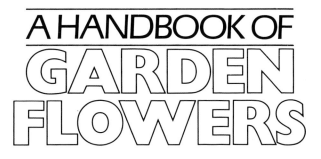

David Papworth • Bob Legge • Noel Prockter

GALLERY BOOKS

An Imprint of W. H. Smith Publishers Inc.
112 Madison Avenue
New York City 10016

A SALAMANDER BOOK

© Salamander Books Ltd. 1990
129/137 York Way,
London N7 9LG,
United Kingdom.

ISBN 0-8317-4234-8

This edition published in 1990 by Gallery Books,
an imprint of W.H. Smith Publishers, Inc.,
112 Madison Avenue, New York, New York 10016.

Gallery Books are available for bulk purchase for sales
promotions and premium use. For details, write or telephone
the Manager of Special Sales, W.H. Smith Publishers, Inc.,
112 Madison Avenue, New York, New York 10016. (212) 532-6600

CREDITS

Introduction written by: David Squire
Editor: Geoff Rogers
Assistant Editor: Lisa Dyer
Designer: Suzanne Baker
Line artwork: Maureen Holt and David Papworth
Filmset: SX Composing Ltd., Essex, England
Color separation: Scantrans Pte Ltd., Singapore

Printed in Belgium by Proost International Book Production

PICTURE CREDITS

The majority of the photographs in this book have been
taken by Eric Crichton. Other photographs are credited
as follows on the page: (B) Bottom, (T) Top.

Pat Brindley: 32(B)
Ralph Gould: 33(T)
David Squire: 22

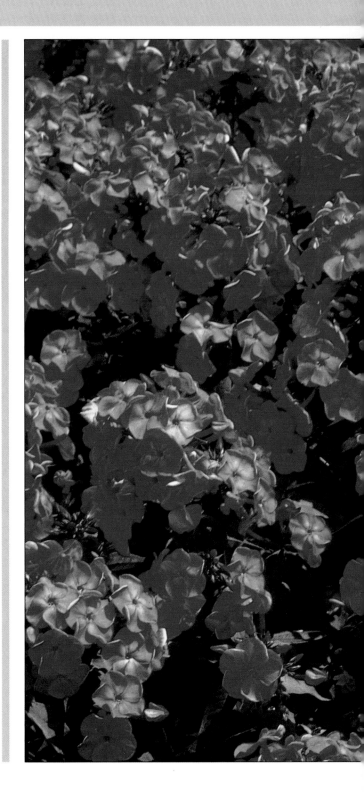

Right: *This lovely purple-red
variety of Phlox paniculata has a
wonderful musky fragrance.*

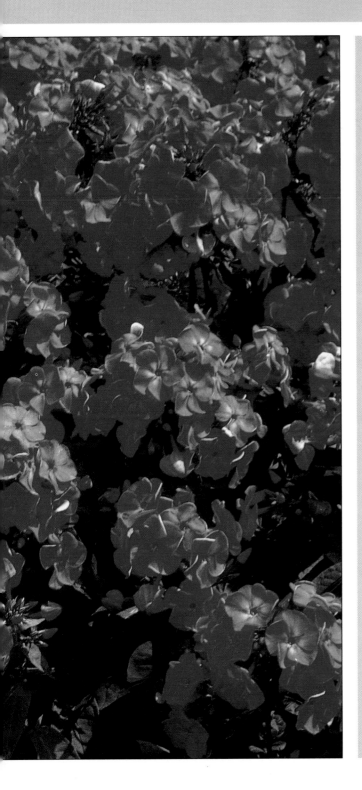

INTRODUCTION

Flower borders ablaze with colour from early spring through to the frosts of autumn are the aim of every gardener. However large or small your garden, there are many plants to choose from to help you to achieve this goal.

The range of flowering plants featured in this colourful book is wide, from hardy annuals which can be sown in spring in their flowering positions to half-hardy types which initially need the warmth of a greenhouse and later can be planted into borders or containers on a patio. There are biennials which are sown in nursery beds one year and bear their flowers during the following season. Other plants have a more perennial nature, such as herbaceous plants which die down to ground-level each autumn and create a fresh array of leaves and flowers the following year. There are also plants with a bulbous nature, including not only true bulbs, such as daffodils and tulips, but also corm-forming types like gladioli. Others have a rhizomatous nature, such as lily-of-the-valley, with slender underground stems. Some irises, such as the large bearded types, also have rhizomes, but these are thicker and only partly buried in soil. Whatever their nature, all of these plants have their own role to play in bringing colour and life to a garden or patio.

Using this book
The garden flowers are arranged in alphabetical order according to their scientific (botanical) names. Unfortunately, some plants are occasionally re-classified and given new names, but the old name may remain in popular use. Each plant in this book has been given the name by which it is usually sold. If it has an alternative scientific name, this is also indicated, as well as any common names. Common names are important to most gardeners because they are often familiar, amusing, and descriptive.

Knowing each plant's individual requirements enables you to produce a healthy and flourishing garden. For most plants there are a few key factors which influence their success, such as the available sunlight, the temperature, the nature of the soil, and the seasons. Each entry includes specific information on these key factors along with information on general care, sowing, planting, cultivation and propagation techniques. Throughout the book some of the most important points have been highlighted under each plant name. Also included is a description of the plant and some of its varieties. The height of each plant is given as well as the best position for the plant in the flower bed.

Using plants in the garden
When planning your garden, consider the plants' requirements for growth as well as how the plants will complement each other. Take into account the growth of a plant and whether one will invade or overshadow another and block natural light.

There are flowers available for all areas of the garden: in a hardy annual border, in herbaceous borders, in mixed borders which are a medley of all plant types, in pots on a patio, in hanging baskets, or in window boxes. No part of your garden need be bare of colour whether it is spring, summer or autumn.

Acanthus mollis

(Artist's acanthus, Bear's breeches)

▶ **Sunny position**
▶ **Well-drained soil**
▶ **Late summer flowering**

This attractive, architectural herbaceous perennial has glossy-green foliage. The mauve-pink, foxglove-like flowers are rather sparingly produced on stems 120cm (48in) or higher. As plants can spread as much as 90cm (36in) and have invasive roots, it is advisable not to grow more than one plant in small gardens. Any good fertile soil suits this acanthus, provided it is well-drained. Plant in spring. During the first winter, especially in cold districts, give a mulch of leaf-mould or well-rotted garden compost.

A. spinosus, the spiny bear's breeches, is similar in many respects, except that it has nasty spines at the end of each dark, deeply divided leaf. Each leaf is about 60-90cm (24-36in) long.

Propagate by seed sown in spring in a cold frame, by root cuttings in late autumn or winter, or by division in spring.

Take care
Protect from frost and drying winds in their first winter.

Achillea filipendulina

(Fern-leaf yarrow, Noble yarrow, Yarrow)

▶ **Sunny position**
▶ **Tolerates dry soils**
▶ **Summer flowering**

The large yellow plate-like flowers of A. filipendulina, an herbaceous perennial, are best seen in the variety 'Gold Plate'. This most spectacular plant has flat, bright yellow heads at the top of stout, erect stems, 150cm (60in) tall. Each flower head can be 13cm (5in) across and the plant can spread as much as 45cm (18in).

Another superb variety is 'Coronation Gold'. This plant has pale yellow flat heads and 90cm (36in) stems which rise out of grey-green feathery foliage.

Propagate by seeds or division in spring, or by cuttings in early summer. Plant in spring in good retentive soil. A few peasticks will be needed to protect the heavy heads in wet weather, particularly in windswept gardens.

The tall varieties should be cut down to ground level during the autumn. The flower heads can be dried for winter decoration indoors.

Take care
Plant this species in a sheltered spot, if possible.

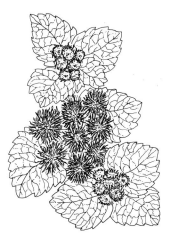

Above: The pale yellow flower heads of Achillea filipendulina 'Coronation Gold' are borne on stout stems up to 90cm (36in) high. Plant this flower in a sheltered spot or provide support.

Right: Ageratum houstonianum 'Adriatic Blue' have neat cushions of fluffy flowers – like shaving brushes. Suitable for carpeting and border edgings and widely grown in summer-bedding schemes.

Left: Both the mauve-pink flowers and glossy-green foliage of the dramatic looking Acanthus mollis are handsome. A single specimen would suit a small garden because its roots can be invasive.

Agapanthus africanus
(Agapanthus umbellatus)
(African blue lily, African lily, Lily of the Nile)

▶ **Sunny position**
▶ **Moist fertile soil**
▶ **Summer flowering**

This flesh-rooted, half-hardy, evergreen border plant was previously known as *Agapanthus umbellatus* and belongs to the family Liliaceae, but is not a lily. It is hardy out of doors only in gardens that are usually frost-free. Today, however, there are some very fine garden forms that are hardy. During the 1950s and 1960s, the 'Headbourne Hybrids' were developed from *A. campanulatus*; they are in varying shades of blue.

All agapanthus plants have lily-like flowers that are arranged in an umbel – like an upturned umbrella. The flowers are borne on stoutish stems, 60-90cm (24-36in) high. It is wise to mark the spot where the plants grow so that, when the border is dug over, the plants are not damaged. Choose moist rather than dry soil, but avoid very wet ground.

Propagate by division in spring, as new growth appears.

Take care
Avoid deep planting.

Ageratum houstonianum
(Flossflower, Pussy-foot)

▶ **Sow in spring**
▶ **Most ordinary types of soil**
▶ **Tolerates all positions except heavy shade**

Flowering from early summer onwards, this beautiful half-hardy annual has flower heads which resemble small powder puffs. Shown to their best when edging a formal bedding scheme, they are also good subjects for window boxes and containers.

Use the F1 hybrids now available; these give larger and longer trusses of blooms. The cultivar 'Adriatic' is in this class: its height is 20cm (8in), and the mid-blue flower is produced above light green hairy leaves. Although most cultivars are in the blue range, there are a few whites available.

Sow seed in boxes of growing medium in spring, under glass. When large enough to handle, prick out in the usual way. Plant out in final positions at the end of spring or when the risk of frost has disappeared. Until planting out, try to maintain a temperature of 10-16°C (50-60°F); lower than this will tend to check growth.

Take care
Avoid planting out too early.

Allium moly
(Golden garlic, Leek lily,
Yellow onion)

▶ **Sunny site**
▶ **Well-drained soil**
▶ **Plant with 7.5cm (3in) of soil
over the bulb**

This bulbous-rooted plant is
suitable for the rock garden, as it
grows only 30cm (12in) tall. It has
strap-like grey leaves and yellow
star-like flowers that form clusters
5cm (2in) wide on the end of the
flower stems in midsummer. The
plants spread and should be
planted 15cm (6in) apart.

Plant the bulbs in autumn in
well-drained soil with some
moisture; they prefer a sunny site.
Leave them for a few years until
the flowers become crowded, then
lift the clump in spring or autumn.
Split and replant with more space.
A. moly can be grown as a pot
plant provided it is kept cool until
the flower buds start to open and
then it can be brought indoors.
Sow seeds in winter or spring.

Protect from slugs and watch for
white rot. If white fungus appears
at the base of the bulbs, destroy
the plants and do not grow alliums
in this soil for 10 years.

Take care
Avoid waterlogged soil.

Alstroemeria aurantiaca
(Lily of the Incas, Peruvian lily)

▶ **Sunny, sheltered site**
▶ **Well-drained fertile soil**
▶ **Plant tubers 10-15cm (4-6in)
deep**

This tuberous-rooted, half-hardy
plant has twisted blue-grey leaves
and grows to a height of 90cm
(36in). Borne on leafy stems, the
flowers are trumpet-shaped in
orange-red with red veins.

Plant the tubers in spring. Cover
with a mulch of compost or well-
rotted manure in spring. As they
grow, support to prevent them
being blown over. Dead-head
plants to encourage more blooms.
In autumn cut stems down to the
ground. In spring the plants can be
divided, but take care not to
disturb the roots unduly.
Sometimes the plant will not
produce any stems, leaves or
flowers during the first season but,
once established, it can be left for
years. Sow seed in spring in a cold
frame and plant out a year later.

Watch for slugs and caterpillars,
using an insecticide if necessary.
When the plant shows yellow
mottling and distorted growth,
destroy it – this is a virus disease.

Take care
Avoid damaging the roots.

*Above: The rich colour and exotic
markings of Alstroemeria
aurantiaca contrast with the blue-
grey leaves in summer. Place this
plant in a sheltered site in full sun.*

*Below: Amaryllis belladonna is an
exotic plant that is ideal in a
sheltered border or among shrubs
where the large blooms make a
fine spectacle in late summer.*

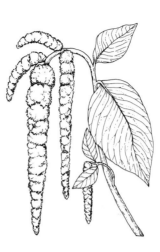

Amaranthus caudatus

(Love-lies-bleeding, Tassel flower)

▶ **Sow in spring**
▶ **Well-cultivated soil**
▶ **Sunny location**

This hardy annual has long, tail-like clusters of crimson flowers which can reach 45cm (18in) in length. The flowers are produced on stems up to 105cm (42in) tall. Leaves are ovate in shape and green in colour, the green changing to bronze as the season progresses. *A. caudatus* is used mainly in formal beds as a 'spot' plant to give height. Try them as individual specimens in largish containers or in groups on a mixed border. The long tassel flowers will appear in summer.

For borders, sow the seed directly into the open ground in a sunny position in spring. When thinning out seedlings, give plenty of room for development – about 60cm (24in) apart.

Raise plants for containers and formal borders by sowing in boxes of good seed-growing medium in early spring. Prick off into individual pots under glass and plant out into their final positions in late spring.

Take care
Keep well-watered in dry periods.

Amaryllis belladonna

(Belladonna lily, Cape belladonna, Naked lady)

▶ **Sunny sheltered position**
▶ **Well-drained soil**
▶ **Plant 15-20cm (6-8in) deep**

This bulbous plant has strap-like leaves, lasting from late winter through to midsummer. After the leaves die down, flower stems appear and grow to a height of 75cm (30in). The trumpet-shaped fragrant pink or white flowers vary from three to 12 on a stem.

Plant the bulbs in summer in a warm, sheltered situation in well-drained soil. Bulbs can be divided in summer and should be replanted immediately. Dead-head the flowers as they fade; remove leaves and stems as they die.

Hippeastrum bulbs, often sold as amaryllis, are tender indoor subjects. Plant one bulb in a 15-20cm (6-8in) pot of well-draining mixture, leaving a third of the bulb exposed. Water a little until the flower stem appears and then water and feed liberally. Bulbs bloom about three months after planting. Prepared bulbs planted in late autumn flower during mid-winter.

Take care
Keep moist when transplanting.

Above: This vigorous plant, Amaranthus caudatus, produces lovely crimson tassels during midsummer. Grow them in groups in a mixed border or singly in containers. Leaves bronze with age.

Anemone × hybrida

(Japanese anemone, Japanese windflower, Windflower)

▶ **Sun or partial shade**
▶ **Good ordinary soil**
▶ **Early autumn flowering**

Of all the many windflowers, the best-known are the many hybrids of the hardy, herbaceous perennial *Anemone × hybrida* (also known as *A. japonica*). These vary in height from 45-120cm (18-48in), and their individual flowers vary in size from 4-6cm (1.6-2.4in) across, each with five or more petals. Each flower has a central boss of yellow stamens. The stems are clothed with vine-like leaves. Their roots are like stiff black leather bootlaces. Choose from the following selection: 'Bressingham Glow', a semi-double rosy red, 45cm (18in) tall; 'Luise Uhink', white, 90cm (36in); 'September Charm', single soft pink, 45cm (18in); 'White Queen', 90-120cm (36-48in); and 'Honorine Jobert', white, 120cm (48in).

Propagate by cutting the roots into 4-5cm (1.6-2in) lengths and inserting them in a deep box filled with peat and sand mixture.

Take care
Good drainage is needed and, preferably, a sunny position.

Antirrhinum majus 'Guardsman'

(Snapdragon)

▶ **Sow late winter/early spring**
▶ **Light to medium soil**
▶ **Sunny position**

Antirrhinums are very popular garden plants, usually grown as half-hardy annuals. Among the many varieties is the 'Guardsman'. It is brilliant scarlet with a white throat and yellow lips to the open parts of the central petals. Growing to a height of 38-45cm (15-18in), this cultivar is very free flowering.

As this is a half-hardy annual, sow seeds in late winter under glass or in early spring in a temperature of 16-18°C (60-65°F). Use a good peat-based growing medium or make up your own (without nutrients) of equal parts of peat and sand. Sow seed thinly and cover only lightly. Seedlings are prone to damping off disease and this is often caused by a too rich growing medium, so beware. Prick off into boxes when large enough to handle. Harden off and plant out in early summer at 23cm (9in) apart.

Take care
Pinch out the central growing point when young plants are 10cm (4in) high; this makes bushier plants.

Far left: *The lovely white Anemone 'Honorine Jobert' was a 'sport' from a red-flowered variety in the garden of M. Jobert in 1858.*

Left: *Aster novi-belgii 'Orlando' has pink-purple flowers which are freely borne on stems up to 150cm (60in) in height during autumn.*

Below: *The large-flowered Aster amellus 'King George' has held its popularity since it was bred in 1914. The soft blue-violet blooms are borne on 60cm (24in) stems.*

Tall variety

Aster amellus

(Italian aster, Italian starwort)

▶ **Sunny position**
▶ **Retentive well-drained soil**
▶ **Late summer and early autumn flowering**

This colourful herbaceous perennial has large solitary flowers with golden-yellow centres and several clusters to each strong branching stem. The grey-green foliage and the stems are rough when handled. These plants form a woody rootstock.

Four varieties to choose from are: 'King George', soft blue-violet 8cm (3.2in) flowers with golden-yellow centres, introduced seventy years ago; the 60cm (24in) tall 'Nocturne', with lavender-lilac flowers; the large-flowered pink 'Sonia', 60cm (24in); and the compact dwarf aster, 45cm (18in) tall, 'Violet Queen'.

They object to winter wetness and are happiest in a good well-drained retentive soil. They are best planted in spring. Propagate by basal cuttings in spring or by division where possible.

Take care
Do not let them have wet rootstocks in winter.

Aster novi-belgii

(Michaelmas daisy, New England aster, Starwort)

▶ **Sunny position**
▶ **Fertile soil**
▶ **Early autumn flowering**

Michaelmas daisies are superb herbaceous perennials with large and colourful daisy-like flower heads in September and October. They need to be grown in fertile soil, as they soon exhaust the ground. Position in full sun.

There are many varieties to choose from; some of these are: 'Carnival' with semi-double, cherry-red flowers 60cm (24in) high; 'Freda Ballard' with semi-double, rich red flowers 90cm (36in) high; and 'Royal Ruby' with semi-double, rich ruby, early flowers 50cm (20in) high.

Dwarf varieties include: 'Jenny' with double red flowers 30cm (12in) high; 'Professor Kippenburg' with clear blue flowers 30cm (12in) high; and 'Snowsprite' with white, late flowers 30cm (12in) high.

Propagate these plants by dividing the roots in spring, every three years. Replant only the healthiest pieces.

Take care
If mildew attacks, spray with flowers of sulphur.

Astilbe × arendsii

(False goat's beard,
Perennial spiraea)

▶ **Sunshine or partial shade**
▶ **Moist fertile soil**
▶ **Summer flowering**

Astilbes are one of the most
decorative hardy herbaceous
perennials. The arendsii hybrids
vary from white, through pale pink,
deep pink, coral and red, to
magenta. Not only are they good
garden plants, but they also force
well under glass in an unheated
greenhouse. The foliage varies
from light to dark green, with some
of purplish and reddish-purple
shades. The fluffy panicles of
flowers are held on erect stems
60-90cm (24-36in) tall, but dwarf
varieties are only 45cm (18in).

They will grow in full sun or
partial shade and thrive in most
soils. They have a long flowering
period and their rigid erect stems
do not require staking. There are
too many varieties to mention, but
all are worth a place in any garden.

Propagate by division in spring.
Alternatively, roots may be divided
in autumn and potted for forcing or
spring planting.

Take care
Do not cut old flower stems back
before spring.

Brachycome iberidifolia

(Swan River daisy)

▶ **Sow in mid-spring**
▶ **Rich soil**
▶ **Sunny but sheltered site**

The daisy flowers of this half-hardy
annual may be lilac, blue-purple,
pink or white. Very free-flowering
and fragrant, the blooms are
produced on compact plants from
early summer onwards. It is very
striking when sited towards the
front of a border and can also be
planted in containers on a sunny
sheltered patio or yard. Wiry stems
reach a height of 45cm (18in) and
carry light green leaves that are
deeply cut. The scented flowers,
when fully open, are about 4cm
(1.6in) across.

Sow the seed under glass in
spring. Use a good, ordinary seed-
growing medium, and maintain a
temperature of 16°C (60°F). When
seedlings are ready, prick off in the
usual way. Set plants out at 35cm
(14in) intervals in late spring.
Alternatively, sow seed directly
into the border during mid-spring
and thin out later. Some support
may be necessary.

Take care
Avoid windy sites.

Above: Astilbe × arendsii are
hardy herbaceous perennials ideal
for a garden where the soil does
not dry out.

Above right: Calendula officinalis
'Lemon Gem' is a reliable annual
which needs sun. It has double
flowers of beautiful yellow
blooming throughout the summer.

Left: Myriads of fragrant daisy
flowers cover the compact
Brachycome iberidifolia during the
summer months. They thrive in sun
but must be sheltered from wind.

Right: Callistephus chinensis
'Milady Dark Rose' is a dwarf type
of China aster bearing large, long-
lasting blooms. An ideal bedding
plant, particularly in windy areas.

Calendula officinalis 'Lemon Gem'
(Pot marigold)
► Sow in early spring or autumn
► Ordinary free-draining soil
► Sunny spot

The very reliable calendulas never cease to delight. The beautiful yellow, orange or gold shades of the flowers are a cheerful sight throughout the season. 'Lemon Gem' has striking double yellow flowers that are formed on compact plants 30cm (12in) high. The long light green leaves are a perfect setting for the bright flowers. Very free-flowering and highly pungent, they can be used almost anywhere in the garden.

As this is a hardy annual, seeds can be sown where they are to flower during the autumn or early spring. Take out shallow drills and then lightly cover the seed. Thin out to 15cm (6in) apart. Alternatively, they can be raised under glass to give uniformity for the formal planting areas. Raise during early spring in a frost-free temperature. Autumn-sown plants will be stronger and flower earlier.

Take care
Dead-head to prolong flowering.

Callistephus chinensis 'Milady Dark Rose'
(Annual aster, China aster)
► Sow in early spring
► Ordinary well-drained soil
► Sunny and open site

China asters are useful plants for a bed or border, or in containers, including window boxes. Recent developments have led to a number of useful additions of the dwarf bedding types, and the cultivar 'Milady Dark Rose' is recommended. The rose-coloured double flowers are borne above the dark green foliage. Plants are about 23cm (9in) high, making them ideal bedding plants especially in areas where wind may cause damage to taller types.

Asters can be affected by various wilt disorders so avoid planting them in the same spot more than once. Sow seed under glass in early spring at a temperature of 16°C (60°F). Use any good growing medium for this purpose, and the subsequent pricking out into boxes. Harden them off in the usual way and plant out into flowering positions in early summer, 15cm (6in) apart.

Take care
Avoid overwatering at any stage.

Campanula lactiflora

(Milky bellflower)

▶ **Full sun**
▶ **Deep fertile soil**
▶ **Early to late summer flowering**

This is a superb herbaceous perennial which will reach a height of 120-150cm (48-60in), and in partial shade may reach 180cm (72in), though it is better in full sun. Its stout stems require staking in windy gardens. The rootstock, although vigorous, fortunately does not rampage in the soil. The rigid stems carry loose or dense panicles of white or pale blue to deep lilac flowers. The stems are clothed with small light green leaves. The flesh-pink 'Loddon Anna' is a lovely form of *C. lactiflora*, 120-150cm (48-60in) tall. The baby of this species, 'Pouffe', only 25cm (10in) high, is an ideal dwarf plant, with light green foliage forming mounds that are smothered for weeks with lavender-blue flowers during the early and midsummer months.

Propagate by division or by cuttings in spring.

Take care
These campanulas need moisture during the growing season.

Canna × hybrida

▶ **Sunny and sheltered position**
▶ **Rich peaty soil**
▶ **Just cover the rhizome**

These tropical plants have broad leaves and bright flowers. The plants grow to a height of 120cm (48in) and should be kept at least 30cm (12in) apart. Cannas fall into two groups, those with green leaves and those with brown to purple ones. The leaves can be up to 60cm (24in) long and 30cm (12in) wide. The flowers are about 7.5cm (3in) long, in brilliant orange or yellow.

Plant the rhizomes in pots in early spring and keep them at 16°C (60°F). If more than one shoot appears, the rhizome can be divided. Make sure that each section has a shoot, a piece of rhizome and some roots. In late spring, they can be planted outside in a sheltered sunny place. Bring plants indoors before autumn frosts, and keep in a cool but not cold place during the winter. Treat soil and plants with a general pesticide to deter slugs, leather-jackets and cutworms. Cannas are usually disease-free.

Take care
Keep frost-free in winter.

Far left: When grouped together in a bed, *Canna × hybrida 'Assault'* forms a fine display, standing over 100cm (39in) in height. The flower heads shine throughout summer.

Left: Both *Centaurea cyanus 'Blue Ball'* and *'Red Ball'* are shown here growing together. Excellent for cutting and ideal for a sunny spot.

Below left: *Campanula lactiflora 'Pouffe'* is a charming miniature campanula. This perennial has little green hummocks covered in lavender-blue flowers.

Below: *Chelone obliqua* is a perennial with unusually shaped flowers that resemble a turtle's head. Do not grow near weaker plants because it will spread.

Centaurea cyanus
(Bachelor's buttons, Bluebottle, Cornflower)

▶ **Sow in autumn or spring**
▶ **Ordinary well-drained soil**
▶ **Sunny position**

The common native cornflower, a hardy annual, is a great favourite, but selection and breeding over many years has led to improved strains for the garden. If you decide to grow this plant, try 'Blue Ball', an attractive blue type. Strong 90cm (36in) stems carry the ball-like flowers well above the leaves, which are narrow and lanceolate in shape. Grow in bold groups near godetias and you will have a beautiful contrast of colour during the summer. They are often grown as cut flowers either on the border or in rows in another part of the garden. 'Red Ball' is another attractive variety.

Sow seeds in either autumn or spring; those sown in autumn will make larger plants. Take out drills where the plants are to flower, sow the seed and cover. Thin out subsequent seedlings to 45cm (18in). In very cold areas, protect autumn-sown seedlings from frost.

Take care
Give support to very tall types.

Chelone obliqua
(Snakehead, Turtlehead)

▶ **Sun; tolerates light shade**
▶ **Fertile well-drained soil**
▶ **Autumn flowering**

This rather strange-looking herbaceous perennial derives its popular name from the unusual shape of its flowers. It is a close relation of the penstemons and is sometimes confused with them. Its dark green leaves are broad to oblong in shape, 5-20cm (2-8in) long, and arranged in pairs, the last two being just below the erect crowded truss of rosy-purple flowers. The square stems are 60-90cm (24-36in) tall. Provided it is given a sunny position in the border, this plant will produce blooms for several weeks in autumn. The flowers are very weather resistant, which is useful in wet seasons. Its roots have a spreading habit.

Propagate by seed sown in spring under glass in a temperature of 13-18°C (55-65°F), or in late spring without heat in a cold frame. Also, propagate by division of roots in spring or in late autumn as soon as flowers fade.

Take care
Chelones may crowd out less tough growing plants.

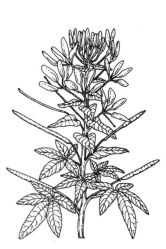

Chrysanthemum maximum

(Shasta daisy)
► **Sunny location**
► **Any good fertile soil**
► **Summer flowering**

The Shasta daisy, a native of the Pyrenees, is a must for any herbaceous perennial border. The height varies from 60 to 90cm (24-36in). Flowers are single or double, with plain or fringed petals. Because of the large flat heads, rain and wind can soon knock plants over. Short peasticks should be inserted in the ground before the plants are too advanced.

One of the best-known varieties is 'Esther Read', 45cm (18in) tall, with pure white, fully double flowers. 'Wirral Pride' is a 90cm (36in) beauty with large anemone-centred blooms and another variety is the fully double white-flowered 'Wirral Supreme', 80cm (32in) high. If you prefer a large, fully double, frilly-flowered variety, plant 'Droitwich Beauty', 80-90cm (32-36in) tall. The creamy-yellow 'Mary Stoker' is 80cm (32in) tall.

Propagate by softwood cuttings in summer, or by division in autumn or spring.

Take care
Be sure to provide support.

Cleome spinosa 'Colour Fountain'

(Spider plant)
► **Sow in spring**
► **Light, ordinary soil**
► **In full sun**

This is a very unusual-looking half-hardy annual; the flowers are spider-shaped and scented. 'Colour Fountain' mixture will include shades of rose, carmine, purple, lilac and pink. Stems reach 60-90cm (24-36in) and carry digitate leaves of five to seven lobes. Some spines may be evident on the undersides of these leaves. This is extremely useful as a 'spot' plant to give height to formal bedding schemes. As a border plant, its height will add character, but care should be taken to position it towards the rear in a sunny place.

To flower in summer, seed will need to be sown under glass in spring. Use a well-recommended growing medium and keep the plant at a temperature of 18°C (65°F). Prick out the seedlings into individual pots, 9cm (3.5in) in diameter. Harden off gradually and plant out in late spring.

Take care
Check for aphids on young plants.

Above: Every garden should contain a clump of these dependable perennials, Chrysanthemum maximum. They tolerate all soils and are available with single or double blooms.

Right: Cleome spinosa 'Colour Fountain' is a spectacular plant which produces clusters of spidery flowers on tall strong stems. It is delicately scented.

Below: Coreopsis tinctoria 'Dwarf Dazzler' is a reliable dwarf cultivar with masses of crimson and gold flowers in summer. This plant will tolerate the polluted atmosphere of towns and cities.

Convallaria majalis
(Lily of the valley)
- ▶ **Light shade or dappled sun**
- ▶ **Retentive fertile soil**
- ▶ **Late spring flowering**

Lily of the valley is one of the best-loved, sweetly scented, herbaceous perennials. It has creeping, spreading rhizomes, and is usually sold by bulb companies. This pretty, shade-loving plant enjoys liberal supplies of humus in the soil. Some sunshine is preferable, provided moisture and humus are available.

Plant in early autumn. The rhizomatous roots should be placed 7.5-10cm (3-4in) beneath the surface, with the fleshy crowns pointing upwards about 2.5cm (1in) under the surface. Keep the ground moist from spring to autumn. A top dressing of rotted farmyard manure, garden compost or leaf-mould should be given annually. When picking, pull the flower stems carefully, leaving a pair of leaves. If you must have leaves, pull only one from each crown. Propagate by division in early autumn.

Take care
The plants must always have plenty of moisture and humus.

Coreopsis tinctoria 'Dwarf Dazzler'
(Calliopsis, Tickseed)
- ▶ **Sow in spring to early summer**
- ▶ **Fertile, well-drained soil**
- ▶ **Sunny location**

This hardy, dwarf annual has beautiful daisy-shaped flowers of deep crimson and each flower is edged with golden yellow, making a vivid contrast. Only 30cm (12in) in height and tending to spread, it is ideally suited to the front of a border or bed in a sunny position. It can also be useful in containers on a patio. An added asset is the remarkable tolerance to smoky environments, and it can therefore be put to good use in industrial towns or cities. Long-lasting and very free-flowering, it should be planted in bold groups to get maximum effect.

Wherever you choose to grow these plants, they come readily from seed. Sow in spring to early summer where they are to flower, take out shallow drills and cover seed lightly. If you make later sowings and the weather is dry, then water regularly. Thin out seedlings to 30cm (12in) when large enough to handle.

Take care
Sow only when conditions allow.

Coreopsis verticillata
(Tickseed)

► **Full sun**
► **Fertile soil**
► **Summer and autumn flowering**

This plant from the eastern United States is one of the best herbaceous perennials for the front of the border. It makes a dense bushy plant. The deep green foliage is finely divided on stiff needle-like stems that support bright yellow starry flowers as much as 4cm (1.6in) across. The blooms have a very long season. The flowers are fine for cutting and mix particularly well with the light lavender-blue flowers of *Aster × frikartii* hybrids. Coreopsis must not be left in the same place too long without being lifted and divided or the plants will become starved. This species does not require support.

There is also an improved and larger-flowered variety called *C. verticillata* 'Grandiflora', which has warmer yellow flowers.

Propagate this plant by division in spring.

Take care
Do not let this plant dry out in warm weather; water in the evening.

Crocosmia masonorum
(Montebretia)

► **Sunny location**
► **Well-drained sandy soil**
► **Plant 7.5cm (3in) deep**

This South African cormous plant has sword-like leaves with pronounced centre spines, and grows to 75cm (30in) tall. The flowers are bright orange, 2.5cm (1in) long, and the plant will give a succession of blooms from midsummer.

These plants can be invasive; confine them by planting in a bottomless container sunk into the ground. The corms should be planted in spring, 7.5cm (3in) deep and 15cm (6in) apart, in a sunny position. The plants need a well-drained soil, but keep it moist during summer droughts. The flowers are often used for cutting; if they are left on the plants, remove them as soon as they die. Cut off dead leaves before the new ones appear in spring. Corms should be lifted every few years; divide after flowering and before new growth appears. They are normally pest- and disease-free.

Take care
Stop plants spreading too far.

eft: Crocosmia masonorum gives continuous display of blooms roughout the summer, provided has plenty of sun and the soil is ot too moist. Its arching stance elps it to merge and harmonize ith nearby plants.

ight: This crocus, Crocus hrysanthus 'Blue Bird', shows a lue bud that opens out to reveal reamy-white inside with a deep range centre. It will thrive in full un in any well-drained soil.

elow: One of the first crocuses to ower, Crocus tomasinianus roduces blooms in late winter. he plant needs some protection give it a good start but will then rive in most areas of the garden.

Crocus chrysanthus 'Blue Bird'

▶ **Sheltered sunny position**
▶ **Well-drained soil**
▶ **Plant 7.5cm (3in) deep**

This spring-flowering crocus has a bloom with a mauve-blue exterior edged with white, a creamy white inside and a deep orange centre. The narrow, green leaves have a pale stripe, and arise from a corm.

These crocuses are ideal for a border or rock garden, and do well in pots in a cold greenhouse. Corms can be planted in any free-draining soil. If the soil is very light, they can be planted 15cm (6in) deep, but otherwise 7.5cm (3in) is recommended. If crocuses are grown in grass, delay mowing until the leaves turn yellow and die back; if you cut sooner, the corms will produce very poor blooms next season. Treat the soil with a general pesticide and fungicide. Mice and birds can be deterred by the use of mouse bait and black cotton stretched over the plants; a cat is also a good deterrent.

Take care
Keep the corms from becoming waterlogged.

Crocus tomasinianus

▶ **Sunny site sheltered against cold winds**
▶ **Ordinary well-drained soil**
▶ **Plant 7.5cm (3in) deep**

This winter-flowering crocus has smaller flowers than the spring crocus – up to 7.5cm (3in) long. The delicate blue-lavender flowers bud in winter and open in very early spring. They naturalize well in grass and sunny borders, given a sheltered position, and also do well in groups under deciduous trees or on rockeries. The varieties available are mostly deep purples such as 'Bar's Purple' and 'Whitewell Purple', but a white variety called 'Albus' is for sale from some specialists.

Corms should be planted 7.5cm (3in) deep, but if the soil is very light and summer cultivation is likely to disturb the roots, they can be planted as deep as 15cm (6in). Do not remove flowers as they die and leave foliage until it can be pulled off. Increase stock by growing the cormlets, which should flower in two years. Treat soil with a pesticide and fungicide.

Take care
Leave flowers and leaves on the plant until leaves turn yellow.

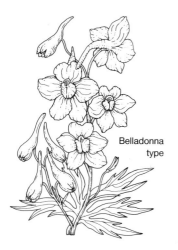

Belladonna type

Delphinium elatum

(Delphinium, Perennial larkspur)

▶ **Full sun**
▶ **Deep rich, well-drained and moisture-retentive soil**
▶ **Summer and autumn flowering**

These are hardy herbaceous perennials, well-known for decorating borders with spires of flowers during June and July. The true species is seldom grown, and the forms now cultivated are *D. elatum* (large-flowered type) and *D. belladonna* types.

The *elatum* plants develop long, upright spires of flowers on plants up to 240cm (96in) high, although dwarf forms, such as 'Baby Doll' and 'Blue Fountains', and medium-height forms, like 'Blue Nile' and 'Cressida', are available.

Derived from the *elatum* are the *belladonna* varieties. They are smaller at between 100-150cm (40-60in) high. They have a lax, graceful habit and beautifully cupped florets.

Propagate these delphiniums by division or by cuttings rooted in a cold frame in spring.

Take care
Avoid cold, wet soils and plant in spring.

Dicentra spectabilis

(Bleeding heart, Dutchman's breeches)

▶ **Partial shade or full sun**
▶ **Rich well-cultivated fertile soil**
▶ **Late spring and early summer flowering**

This charming herbaceous perennial has a fragile look. The glaucous, finely divided foliage has attractive arching sprays off the stoutish stems, about 60cm (24in) high, sometimes taller, from which dangle crimson and white lockets. When open, the flowers are rosy pink with white tips. It makes a good cut flower, and roots potted in autumn can be forced into flower in an unheated greenhouse.

These delicate-looking plants can be damaged by late spring frosts and it is advisable to plant them where the sun does not reach the plants before the frost has gone. Plant *D. spectabilis* where it can be protected by a wall or evergreen shrubs. A mulch of leaf-mould or well-rotted compost should be given each spring.

Propagate in spring by cutting the roots with a sharp knife, or by root cuttings taken in spring and rooted in an unheated frame.

Take care
Protect against wind and frost.

Above: Dictamnus albus has spikes of fragrant white flowers which appear in early summer above the finely divided foliage.

Left: Delphinium 'Thunderstorm' is an elatum type delphinium which develops long spires of intense deep blue flowers during midsummer. It is an ideal perennial for bringing height and focal points to a border.

Dictamnus albus
(Burning bush, Dittany, Fraxinella, Gas plant)

▶ **Full sun**
▶ **Well-drained deep fertile soil**
▶ **Early summer flowering**

The burning bush is an herbaceous perennial, and so called because on hot dry days, when the seedpods are ripening, it is possible by holding a lighted match at the base of the flower stalk to ignite the volatile oil given off by the plant without doing any damage to the dictamnus itself.

The smooth, divided, light green leaves are on erect stems that are lemon scented. The stems bear white flowers that have very long stamens. The plant usually seen in gardens is *D. albus purpureus*, which has soft mauve-purple flowers, veined with red. Both are 90cm (36in) tall. As the plants are deep rooted, they can remain in one place for a number of years.

Propagate by root cuttings in late autumn or winter, or by division in spring.

Take care
Give water in very dry weather.

Didiscus caeruleus
(Trachymene caeruleum)
(Blue lace flower, Queen Anne's lace)

▶ **Sow in spring**
▶ **Ordinary well-cultivated soil**
▶ **Sheltered and sunny position**

This lovely half-hardy annual from Australia – now often called *Trachymene caeruleum* – has the appearance of the perennial scabious. Clusters of delicate lavender-blue flowers are carried on stems 45cm (18in) high. The umbrella-shaped flower head will appear in midsummer and carry on flowering until autumn. Leaves and stems are covered with masses of tiny hairs and feel rough to the touch. Choose a sheltered position, preferably towards the front of a border near annuals with white or pale yellow flowers.

Sowing should be carried out during spring under glass, in a temperature of 16°C (60°F). Use a loam-based growing medium for both seed and seedlings. When large enough to handle, the latter will respond better if pricked out into small individual pots. After hardening off, plant 23cm (9in) apart, near the end of spring.

Take care
Water well in dry periods.

Right: *This Echinops humilis is a variety called 'Veitch's Blue'. It is a coarse, prickly foliaged plant which is festooned with blue globular flowers in late summer. It is easy to grow in full sun.*

Far right: *This original Californian annual, Eschscholzia californica, has been developed into a wide selection of forms and colours. All are best suited for dry and sunny places. Clear self-sown seedlings.*

Below: *Eranthis hyemalis is a ground-hugging plant with brilliant yellow flowers which look like buttercups and appear in mid-winter if conditions are mild. It thrives in a heavy moist soil.*

Echinops humilis 'Taplow Blue'

(Globe thistle, Steel globe thistle)
► **Full sun**
► **Any soil**
► **Late summer flowering**

Globe thistles are herbaceous perennials with round drumstick heads in varying tones of blue. They are coarse growing. Attached to the stout rough wiry stems is deeply cut, greyish, spiny foliage, woolly beneath. Bees are especially attracted to the globular flowers. The flower heads can be dried for winter decoration. The variety 'Taplow Blue' is 150cm (60in) tall with dark blue globular flowers that have a metallic steely lustre. A variety with a slightly richer blue is 'Veitch's Blue'.

These hardy herbaceous perennials can be grown successfully in the poorest of soils, whether sand or chalk, but should be well-drained.

Propagate by root cuttings in late autumn or winter, or by division in autumn or spring.

Take care
Provide a good depth of soil, as the thong-like roots of this plant are very penetrating.

Eranthis hyemalis

(Common winter aconite, Winter aconite)
► **Sun or partial shade**
► **Well-drained heavy soil**
► **Plant 2.5cm (1in) deep**

This European tuberous-rooted plant grows to a height of 10cm (4in) with a spread of 7.5cm (3in). The leaves are pale green and deeply cut. The bright yellow flowers appear in late winter but in mild winters the flowers may start blooming in mid-winter. The flowers are about 2.5cm (1in) across and look like buttercups but with a collar of pale green leaves just below the flower.

Plant tubers in a well-drained soil that is moist throughout the year – a heavy loam is ideal. Grow them in either sun or light shade. To propagate, lift the eranthis when the leaves die down. Break or cut the tubers into sections and replant these immediately, at least 7.5cm (3in) apart. Seed can be sown in spring and kept in a cold frame; transplant in two years and flowering will start after another year. If sooty eruptions occur on the plant, destroy it to stop the spread of smut disease.

Take care
Keep soil moist in spring.

Eschscholzia californica
(Californian poppy)

▶ **Sow in autumn or spring**
▶ **Most soils, including those considered poor**
▶ **Sunny and dry position**

In mild regions, self-seeding of this hardy annual will produce many plants, but, if kept under control, they are an asset to any garden. Nearly always grown as a border plant, they can be used in the rock garden to good advantage. Choose a sunny position for the best results. Flowers are red, yellow, white, pink and orange. Stems carry deeply cut blue-green leaves. The flower buds have a whorled spike effect and, when opened, the petals are silky in texture. Double hybrids are well worth a try and their frilled blooms are an added attraction. Plants will be 30cm (12in) tall.

Sow in flowering positions in autumn for the best results; the plants that winter through will be stronger and flower earlier. Sow also in spring. In both cases, thin seedlings to 15cm (6in) apart.

Take care
Discard self-sown seedlings at the end of summer.

Filipendula purpurea
(Spiraea palmata)
(Dropwort, Meadowsweet)

▶ **Sun or partial shade**
▶ **Cool moist conditions**
▶ **Summer flowering**

This Japanese hardy herbaceous perennial is one of half a dozen dropworts. It can still be found in some nursery catalogues and garden centres under its old name, *Spiraea palmata*. This is a most handsome plant, and if it has moist soil or is growing near the side of a pond, it will not fail to attract attention. It has large, lobed leaves and above the elegant, leafy, crimson stems are large flat heads bearing many tiny carmine-rose flowers, each stem reaching a height of 60-120cm (24-48in). The pinkish *F. rubra* has large flower heads up to 28cm (11in) across. In damp soil, it will form huge clumps, in either sun or shade.

To obtain the best results, grow this plant in partial shade and in rich, fertile, moist soil. Propagate by seeds sown in pans or boxes under glass in autumn, or by division in autumn.

Take care
Make sure that this plant does not lack moisture.

Fritillaria imperialis
(Crown imperial)

► **Full or partial shade**
► **Well-drained soil**
► **Plant 20cm (8in) deep**

This bulbous plant grows up to
90cm (36in) tall, with a centre stem
on which is carried a series of
narrow, pointed, glossy leaves to
half the total height. The top half of
this stem carries a circle of large
beautiful drooping flowers about
5cm (2in) long with a crown of
leaves. The range of bloom colour
is yellow, orange and red.

The bulb should be planted in
autumn in a rich well-drained soil
in shade, preferably where it can
be left undisturbed. Handle bulbs
carefully and do not let them dry
out. Plant the bulb on its side to
stop water getting into the hollow
crown and rotting the bulb. In
heavy soil, a handful of coarse
sand around the bulb will speed
drainage. Cut the stems down
when they die off in summer. Seed
will not produce flowering bulbs for
six years. It is quicker to use
offsets taken from the parent bulb
in late summer; plant in a nursery
bed for two years, then transplant
them to the flowering position.

Take care
Do not bruise or dry the bulb.

Galanthus nivalis
(Snowdrop)

► **Partial shade**
► **Rich well-drained soil**
► **Plant 10-15cm (4-6in) deep**

Snowdrop leaves are flat, sword-
shaped and often blue-green in
colour. The flowers are either
single or double, in white with
green markings on the inner petals,
and can be as long as 2.5cm (1in).
Snowdrops' time of flowering
normally starts around mid-winter.
One variety of this bulbous plant
flowers in late autumn, before the
leaves appear. They can grow up
to 20cm (8in) tall in rich soil and in
partial shade.

The bulbs should be planted
10cm (4in) deep in heavy soil, or
15cm (6in) deep in light soil, in
autumn. The soil should be moist
but well-drained. Move bulbs after
they have finished flowering, while
the soil is moist. Seed may take
five years to bloom, so it is better
to split clusters of bulbs and
spread them out. Take care when
lifting not to damage the roots or
to let them dry out. Use a soil
insecticide and fungicide.

Take care
Leave bulbs undisturbed for
several years for improved
flowering.

ft: Fritillaria imperialis is a most
usual and impressive plant with
oping flowers and a crown of
ves on a tall stem. It needs a
ady or partially shady situation
d a well-drained soil to thrive.

ght: In full sun and a moist soil,
ltonia candicans will reward the
ower with scented blooms
roughout the summer. Reaching
er 100cm (39in) in height, the
ltonia is best suited to the back
the flower border.

low: Normally flowering in mid-
nter, the low-growing snowdrop
lanthus nivalis is often regarded
the herald of spring. It will grow
st in light shade and a good soil
at is moist and free-draining.
ndle bulbs with care.

Galtonia candicans
(Summer hyacinth)

▶ **Full sun**
▶ **Moist well-drained soil**
▶ **Plant 15cm (6in) deep**

This bulbous plant grows up to
120cm (48in), with narrow, sword-
like, pointed leaves 75cm (30in)
long. The dozen or so scented
flowers appear in late summer on a
single stem. They are bell-shaped,
almost 5cm (2in) long, and white in
colour with green markings at the
tip and base of the petals.

The large round bulbs should be
grouped and planted in spring in a
rich well-drained soil. They are
hardy in the more temperate areas
but, where there are hard frosts, it
is better to treat galtonias as pot
plants. As pot plants they should
be started in autumn in order to
flower late the following spring, but
keep them at a temperature of not
less than 4°C (39°F) for success.
Seed takes up to five years to
flower, but offsets taken in autumn
will flower in two years. Treat the
soil with slug bait around the
plants and spray with fungicide to
control grey mould, especially with
newly planted bulbs.

Take care
Protect from severe frost by
covering with bracken or mulch.

Geranium pratense 'Johnson's Blue'
(Crane's-bill, Meadow crane's-bill)

▶ **Sunny position**
▶ **Fertile well-drained soil**
▶ **Early summer flowering**

This geranium is a most
captivating herbaceous perennial.
Above the elegantly divided foliage
that covers the ground, the wiry
30-35cm (12-14in) stems carry
lavender-blue, cup-shaped flowers
with darker veins. The flowers are
produced profusely from early
summer onwards; each measures
up to 5cm (2in) across. A second
flush of these lovely blooms can be
encouraged by cutting down old
flowering stems. A border of this
plant in front of a hedge of white
floribunda roses looks particularly
stunning.

Provided this and other
geraniums have good ordinary soil
and good drainage, very little else
is needed. Plant in autumn or
spring, five plants to the square
metre (square yard). Protect young
plants from the ravages of slugs.
Propagate by division of roots in
autumn or spring.

Take care
Give geraniums good drainage.

Gladiolus (Large-flowered)

(Sword lily)
▶ Full sun
▶ Ordinary garden soil with added humus
▶ Plant 10-15cm (4-6in) deep

The large-flowered gladiolus hybrids are half-hardy cormous plants that need some protection against frost. The plants often reach 120cm (48in) high. The flower spike is about 50cm (20in) long and individual blooms are 17.5cm (7in) across. They flower in summer, in vivid shades of white, yellow, orange, red, purple, rust, pink and mauve, either with markings or plain.

These hybrids are easily grown from corms planted 10-15cm (4-6in) deep. In lighter soils, plant at the greater depth. Put some sharp sand under the corms to aid drainage, and place in full sun. An ordinary garden soil with some manure added is ideal. As they mature, the plants may become top-heavy, so staking is useful. When the plant dies back, lift it and store the new corm in a frost-free place for the following year.

Take care
Protect against frost and excessive wetness.

Gypsophila paniculata

(Chalk plant, Baby's breath)
▶ Sunny location
▶ Well-drained, preferably limy, soil
▶ Summer flowering

The flower heads of this perennial are a mass of small feathery flowers, white or pink. The glaucous leaves are also small. The branching flower heads are used by flower arrangers to add a light cloud effect to floral arrangements. *G. paniculata* 'Bristol Fairy' is the best double form, at 90cm (36in) tall.

As gypsophilas are deep-rooted, the ground must be well prepared before planting; it should be double dug. To do this, take out the first spit or spade's depth of soil, break up the bottom spit with a fork and fill up with the next top spit. Also enrich the ground with well-rotted farmyard manure or well-rotted garden compost. Provided they have full sun and well-drained soil, gypsophilas should be no trouble.

Propagate 'Bristol Fairy' by taking softwood cuttings in late spring to very early summer.

Take care
Insert a few peasticks for support.

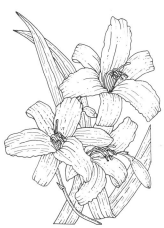

Far left: *A magnificent display of feathery white flowers covers Gypsophila paniculata in midsummer. Needs well-prepared soil and full sunshine to become established.*

Left: *Helianthus annuus 'Sungold' is a low-growing sunflower, especially admired by children. It has 15cm (6in) double blooms.*

Below: *The pink lily-like blooms of Hemerocallis 'Pink Damask' are carried on stems up to 75cm (30in) in height. Allow these plants to grow undisturbed in good soil.*

Helianthus annuus 'Sungold'

(Common sunflower, Mirasol, Sunflower)
- ▶ **Sow in spring**
- ▶ **Ordinary soil**
- ▶ **Sunny position**

So many people grow the giant types of this hardy annual that it is often forgotten that a number of the same sunflowers have dwarf counterparts.

'Sungold', only 60cm (24in) tall, can have a worthy place in any border as long as it can benefit from a sunny position. The beautiful double golden-yellow blooms can be up to 15cm (6in) across, and almost ball-shaped. The short stems and longish leaves feel coarse to the touch and the leaves have toothed margins. More showy when grown in groups, they are best suited to the front of a bed.

Sow seed directly into the ground where they are to flower, putting three seeds to a station. When germination is complete, discard the two weakest seedlings, leaving only the strongest. Spacing should be 30cm (12in).

Take care
Check carefully for slug damage at germination time.

Hemerocallis

(Day lily)
- ▶ **Sun or partial shade**
- ▶ **Any soil but avoid dry ones**
- ▶ **Summer flowering**

Day lilies are hardy herbaceous perennials with large clumps producing an abundance of bright green arching foliage and a display of scented lily-like flowers over a long period. The flowers of early day lilies lasted for only one day, but modern varieties last two or sometimes three days. The lily-like flowers are carried at the top of stout 90cm (36in) stems.

Three modern varieties are: 'Pink Damask', with pretty pink flowers, 75cm (30in) tall; 'Hyperion', with scented, canary-yellow flowers on plants 100cm (40in) high; and the glowing bright red 'Stafford', 75cm (30in) high.

Propagate day lilies by division in spring. Plants can be left undisturbed for many years. Lift and divide them only when clumps become overcrowded.

Take care
In very hot dry weather, give plants a thorough soaking.

Iberis umbellata
(Candytuft, Common candytuft, Globe candytuft)

▶ **Sow from spring onwards**
▶ **Ordinary or poor soil**
▶ **Sunny situation**

Many gardeners will recall the hardy annual candytuft as among the first plants that they grew in a small plot as children. Still very popular, this strongly aromatic annual looks good along the edge of a well-used pathway where its scent can be appreciated. Use it also in bold drifts towards the front of a border.

Umbrella-shaped flowers form in clusters up to 5cm (2in) across, on stems 15-38cm (6-15in) high, from early summer to autumn. The colours are purple, rose-red and white. Leaves are green, lanceolate and slender-pointed, and may be smothered by the profusion of blooms. As flowering is quick from seed, successive sowings will help to prolong the season of flowering.

Sow thinly in spring where they are to flower. Seedlings should be thinned to 15cm (6in) spacing. It is essential to carry out this process correctly if overcrowding and losses are to be avoided.

Take care
Keep removing dead flowers.

Ipheion uniflorum
(Spring starflower)

▶ **Full sun**
▶ **Ordinary soil with good drainage**
▶ **Plant 5cm (2in) deep**

These bulbous plants are noted for their grass-like, sea-green leaves and star-shaped flowers. The plants grow only 20cm (8in) tall, with spring flowers 5cm (2in) wide. The white to deep lavender-blue blooms are scented.

Bulbs should be planted in autumn. Plants should be kept weeded. When leaves and flower stems die back in summer, they should be removed. Position plants in full sun in well-drained soil. The bulbs are increased by bulblets. The plants should be lifted in autumn, divided, and replanted at once. Do this every two or three years to keep the plants free-flowering and healthy. Make sure bulbs do not dry out or become wet during transplanting, and keep the time out of the soil to the minimum. Ipheions are generally trouble-free provided the soil is kept free-draining.

Take care
Do not let bulbs dry out or get wet when planting or transplanting.

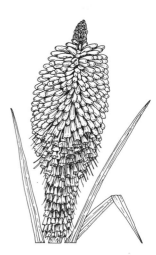

bove: The highly fragrant flowers *f Iberis umbellata* develop *uickly. Successive sowings will nsure a long season of colour at e front of the border. These very opular plants will grow and flower ell on ordinary or poor soils.

eft: Ipheion uniflorum 'Violaceum' a spring-flowering plant which as star-shaped scented blooms. 'his plant is ideal for planting 'ong the front of a border or in a rge rock garden.

ight: Kniphofia praecox is a tall ariety which grows up to 210cm 4in) tall. The magnificent spikes f tubular crimson flowers make a e display in late summer and arly autumn. It creates a ominant feature in a border.

Iris reticulata

▶ **Light shade or sun**
▶ **Light well-drained limy soil**
▶ **Plant 5-7.5cm (2-3in) deep**

These hardy Asian bulbous plants have a net of fibres around the outside of the bulb and grass-like tubular leaves that are dark green with a paler tip. They are early flowering; some start at mid-winter and others follow successively through to spring. The flowers are often 7.5cm (3in) wide, in lemon-yellow and blue. These plants are small and ideal for the rock garden; they rarely grow more than 15cm (6in) tall.

Plant them in a light, well-drained chalky soil. If the ground is heavy, the bulb may not shoot after the first year. Give each bulb a covering of 5-7.5cm (2-3in) of soil. They do best when planted in autumn. After flowering give a liquid feed every four weeks until the bulb dies back. If grown for indoor decoration, plant them in pots. Keep them in a cool temperature until the flower buds show, then bring into the warmth. Use a fungicide and pesticide to keep the plants healthy.

Take care
Do not plant in heavy moist soil.

Kniphofia
(Poker plant, Red-hot poker, Torch lily)

▶ **Full sun**
▶ **Rich retentive well-drained soil**
▶ **Early summer to autumn flowering**

Kniphofias are herbaceous perennials that will come through most winters. To ensure their safety, tie the foliage into a kind of wigwam in winter, to keep the crowns dry. The flowers are carried on stout stems. One beauty is 'Little Maid' about 60cm (24in) tall, with attractive creamy flower spikes. *K. galpinii* 'Bressingham Seedlings' produce orange spikes, 45-90cm (18-36in) tall.

Kniphofias require a fairly rich soil with ample humus such as rotted manure or garden compost. After clumps have been divided, do not allow them to dry out before or after planting. A mulch of rotted manure or garden compost should be given annually in spring, otherwise they can remain untouched for several years. Plant them three or four to the square metre (square yard). Propagate by division in spring.

Take care
Protect crowns during winter.

Lavatera trimestris 'Silver Cup'

(Mallow)

▶ **Sow in autumn or spring**
▶ **Ordinary soil**
▶ **Sunny and sheltered spot**

Mallows have long been grown for their attractive free-flowering effects. The annual cultivar 'Silver Cup' recommended here is one of a number of new hybrids recently developed from *L. rosea*. Glowing pink blooms 7.5-10cm (3-4in) in diameter are freely produced on stems 60-70cm (24-28in) high and spreading to 75cm (30in). This plant is a member of the hollyhock family, and its leaves are green, ovate and lobed. Flowers grow from the leaf axils and are trumpet-shaped, almost satin in texture, and very pleasing to the eye. Apart from their use in the perennial border, try them towards the back of an annual border.

Sow seed directly where plants are to flower, in autumn or spring, and cover lightly. Thin out the seedlings of either sowing during late spring to 45cm (18in) intervals. The strong low branching habit of this plant requires no staking.

Take care
Give plants plenty of space.

Lilium regale

(Regal lily, Royal lily)

▶ **Full sun**
▶ **Well-drained garden soil**
▶ **Plant just below the surface**

This lily originates from China, is very popular and probably the best-known of all lilies. The scented, white, funnel-shaped flowers are up to 12.5cm (5in) long and bloom in summer. The centres of the flowers are brilliant yellow and the backs of the petals have red-purple shading. These lilies can reach 180cm (72in) but most grow to 120cm (48in) tall.

Regal lilies require placement in full sun in a well-drained soil, with or without lime, and they will spread quickly. The bulbs should be planted just below the surface. Some experts recommend planting as deep as 23cm (9in), but this is advisable only in a very light and free-draining soil. Bulbs can be lifted, divided and replanted during the winter months, without letting them dry out. Seeds take up to three years to reach maturity, and most people prefer to grow lilies from bulbs. In exposed areas, stake to prevent wind damage.

Take care
Keep the bulbs moist when planting or transplanting.

Above left: Lavatera trimestris 'Silver Cup' is a fine hybrid for the garden border or for cutting. Sow this plant in spring or autumn and space it out well.

Above: Lobelia erinus 'Colour Cascade Mixed' is a pleasing blend of trailing varieties for hanging baskets, window boxes and low walls. Grow in full sun and give a weak liquid feed every ten days to sustain flowering.

Below left: A hardy and popular lily is Lilium regale. It enjoys full sun and ordinary soil. Do not crowd other plants around it as this detracts from its beauty. Scented flowers in summer.

Left: These Russell lupins, Lupinus polyphyllus 'Russell Hybrids', provide a good mixture of colours for the garden on stems up to 120cm (48in) tall. Grow them on acid or neutral soil.

Lobelia erinus 'Colour Cascade Mixed'

(Edging lobelia, Lobelia)
▶ **Sow in late winter or early spring**
▶ **Ordinary well-cultivated soil**
▶ **Sun or partial shade**

Probably one of the most widely grown half-hardy annuals, lobelia is very versatile. It includes many shades of blue, rose, red, mauve and white eyed flowers, which continue to appear until cut down by autumn frosts.

Although best results are obtained from planting in sunny positions, lobelias also succeed in partial shade. These tender perennials need to be sown in heat in late winter or early spring to obtain maximum results. Sow the small seeds very thinly on the surface of a moistened peat-based seed mixture and do not cover. Germinate in a temperature of 18-21°C (65-70°F). Water carefully to avoid disturbance. Prick out as soon as the seedlings can be handled. Grow on in cooler conditions when established and harden off to plant out when risk of frost has passed.

Take care
Keep the plants watered in dry weather and fed at intervals.

Lupinus polyphyllus

(Lupin, Lupine)
▶ **Sun or light shade**
▶ **Light sandy loam**
▶ **Early summer flowering**

Lupins enjoy sun and well-drained soil. Take care to avoid lime and heavy wet clay soils. Before planting, see that the ground is well cultivated, with an ample supply of well-rotted farmyard manure or garden compost. On well-drained soils, plant in autumn; otherwise, wait until spring.

With established plants, restrict the number of flower spikes to between five and seven, when stems are about 30cm (12in) high. Give a light spraying of plain water in the evening during dry springs. As a rule, staking is not necessary. Named varieties can be obtained, but the Russell hybrids have a good mixture of colours and vary in height from 90 to 120cm (36-48in). In very windy gardens, sow the dwarf 'Lulu' lupin. This is only 60cm (24in) tall.

Propagate by basal cuttings in early spring, when 7.5-10cm (3-4in) long; insert in a cold frame.

Take care
Remove faded flower heads to prevent them forming seeds which will take strength from the plant.

Matthiola incana 'Giant Imperial Mixed'

(Gillyflower, Stock)

▶ **Sow in early spring**
▶ **Most soils, preferably alkaline**
▶ **Sunny position, but tolerates partial shade**

Stocks must be one of the most popular scented annuals. *En masse* this fragrance can be overpowering, however, so do not overplant. The 'Giant Imperial mixture' always provides reliable flowers with a high percentage of doubles. Stems 38-50cm (15-20in) tall carry a profusion of pink, white, lilac, purple and crimson spikes of flowers from early summer onwards. Grey-green soft narrow leaves are formed under the flower heads and give a pleasing and attractive contrast.

Sow seed for summer flowering during the early spring under glass in a temperature of 13°C (55°F). Use a loam-based mixture for sowing and pricking off seedlings. Grow on in a lower temperature and harden off before planting out 23cm (9in) apart.

Take care
Kill caterpillars at once.

Narcissus

(Daffodil)

▶ **Light shade**
▶ **Moist well-drained soil**
▶ **Plant 7.5-10cm (3-4in) deep**

These are the bulbous plants which create a carpet of colour every spring. Daffodils are an important part of the genus Narcissus, but, because they have large trumpets, as long or longer than the surrounding petals, they are known as daffodils. It is not only the daffodils which are worthy of a place in a garden. Others include the diminutive 'Hoop Petticoat' (*Narcissus bulbocodium*), the 'Bunch-flowered Narcissus' (*N. tazetta*), and the 'Angel's Tears' (*N. triandrus albus*).

Daffodils have been classified according to the sizes of their trumpets: if there is one flower (or more) on a stem, if flowers are double or single, and so on. The largest flowering types include: 'Golden Harvest', golden-yellow; 'King Alfred', long-lasting and bright yellow; and 'Arctic Gold', free-flowering and golden.

Take care
Allow the leaves to die down naturally – do not cut them off.

Above: Matthiola incana 'Giant Imperial Mixed' is a fine mixture of these sweetly scented plants. The flowering stems will grow to a height of about 50cm (20in).

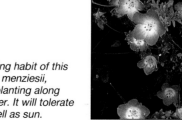

Right: The spreading habit of this annual, Nemophila menziesii, makes it ideal for planting along the edge of a border. It will tolerate partial shade as well as sun.

Nemophila menziesii
(Nemophila insignis)
(Baby blue eyes)

▶ **Sow in spring**
▶ **Ordinary but moist soil**
▶ **Sun or partial shade**

This is one of the more notable hardy annuals from California. Plants grow to a height of 23cm (9in) and have spreading slender stems on which deeply cut, feathery, light green leaves are carried. Appearing from early summer, the flowers are buttercup-shaped and of a beautiful sky blue with a very striking white centre. Each bloom measures 4cm (1.6in) in diameter. This species will tolerate partial shade; use it where a low planting is required.

Before sowing, fork in organic matter if your soil is on the light side. This will ensure that moisture is retained in hot dry spells so that plants can survive. Sow seeds directly where they are to flower, in early spring. Take out shallow drills and only lightly cover the seed. Thin out seedlings to 15cm (6in) apart. In mild regions, autumn sowings will provide plants for flowering in late spring.

Take care
Water freely during dry weather.

Nerine bowdenii

▶ **Sunny position**
▶ **Ordinary well-drained soil**
▶ **Plant just under the surface**

Nerine bowdenii, a half-hardy bulbous plant from South Africa, is sufficiently hardy to withstand most winters in the temperate zone. It will grow to a height of 60cm (24in). The blooms open in autumn, with up to eight flowers in each cluster. The clusters are 15cm (6in) across, usually rose or deep pink, but there is also a white form. The mid-green leaves are narrow and strap-like.

The bulbs should be planted in either late summer or early spring, in an ordinary well-drained soil and in a sunny position. The bulbs are placed just under the surface or, if the soil is light, they can be set deeper – as much as 10cm (4in). Where there are bulbs near the surface, they should be covered with a thick layer of bracken, leaf-mould or compost to protect them against frost. They can be lifted in spring, divided and replanted to encourage larger blooms. Watch for mealy bugs and treat them with pesticide.

Take care
Keep moist when growing.

Above: Nerine bowdenii is a fine showy plant which bears lovely, deep pink flowers in the autumn.

It enjoys a warm sunny border backed with a wall for protection against cold winds and frosts.

Nicotiana × sanderae 'Nicki Hybrids' F1

(Sweet-scented tobacco plant, Tobacco plant)

▶ **Sow in early spring**
▶ **Rich well-drained soil**
▶ **Sun or partial shade**

The Nicki F1 Hybrids are a lovely mixture of colours including red, pink, rose, lime green and white. Individual blooms are up to 6cm (2.4in) long, formed into loose clusters. Stems bearing the flowers carry large oblong leaves of a light green. This strain is dwarf and reaches only about 25cm (10in) in height. The blooms of this free-flowering half-hardy annual are sweetly fragrant. Use as a bedding plant for formal beds or borders, beneath a window, or on a patio or yard where the scent can be appreciated, especially in the evening hours.

Sow seeds under glass in early spring, in a temperature of 18°C (65°F). Seeds should be scattered thinly on top of prepared pots or boxes of a peat-based growing medium. Prick out in the usual way. Harden off and plant out in early summer, 23cm (9in) apart.

Take care
Do not plant out too early.

Ornithogalum umbellatum

(Common star of Bethlehem, Dove's-dung, Nap-at-noon, Star of Bethlehem)

▶ **Partial shade**
▶ **Ordinary well-drained soil**
▶ **Plant 7.5cm (3in) deep**

This bulbous plant grows to a height of 30cm (12in) with a spread of up to 20cm (8in). In spring, the flower stem carries a profusion of white star-like blooms with green stripes on the outside. The plant is hardy and ideal for edgings and mass effects, even naturalizing in short grass or in shrubberies.

Plant the bulbs in autumn, in ordinary well-drained soil with 7.5cm (3in) of soil over them in an area where there is some shade. If possible, dig in a good quantity of peat, compost or leaf-mould beforehand. Once planted, they need no attention and will continue to produce masses of blossom. To increase stock, lift the clumps of bulbs in late summer after the leaves have died down, divide them, and replant with more space. Seeds can be sown, but take up to four years to reach flowering size. Most plants are pest-free, but watch for fungus.

Take care
Keep plants moist in droughts.

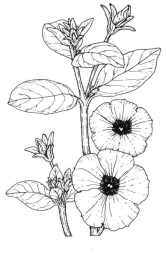

Above: Nicotiana 'Nicki Hybrids' is a colourful mixture of fragrant blooms borne on dwarf plants. Try planting these under a window for heady scents indoors in summer.

Far left: Paeonia officinalis 'Rubra Plena' is an old favourite among peonies. It has large heads of double crimson blooms on stems up to 60cm (24in) tall.

Left: A lovely, free-flowering hybrid, Petunia × hybrida 'Resisto Rose' F1 is ideal for planting in borders or in containers on patios.

Paeonia officinalis 'Rubra Plena'

(Old double crimson, Peony)
▶ **Full sun or partial shade**
▶ **Rich well-drained soil**
▶ **Late spring flowering**

'Rubra Plena' is a beautiful old peony, introduced in the sixteenth century. The large heads of double blooms are held above deeply cut foliage on stems 45-60cm (18-24in) high. Apart from 'Rubra Plena' there is the white 'Alba Plena' and the larger flowered, light pink 'Rosea Superba Plena'.

Peonies are herbaceous perennials and will grow in full sun or partial shade. Choose a site where the plants will not catch the early morning sun, as frosts can injure flower buds. When preparing the site, incorporate well-rotted farmyard manure, garden compost or leaf-mould. An application of liquid manure as the buds start to swell will be beneficial. A feed of bonemeal and a mulch of humus should be worked into the soil every autumn.

Propagate by division in early autumn or in early spring before new growth starts.

Take care
See that plants have enough moisture in dry weather.

Petunia × hybrida

▶ **Sow in early spring**
▶ **Ordinary well-cultivated soil**
▶ **Sunny location**

In a good sunny summer, the petunia is second to none for its profusion of colour and versatility of use. Flowers are trumpet-shaped, up to 10cm (4in) across. Leaves and stems will be a mid to dark green. Leaves vary in size but are usually ovate. The whole plant feels sticky to the touch. Use these petunias for a range of purposes including formal bedding, borders, containers, window boxes and hanging baskets.

Petunias are really half-hardy perennials, but are invariably grown as half-hardy annuals. All petunias love a sunny position and benefit from being grown in a well-cultivated soil. Avoid having the soil over-rich, as this can lead to a lot of growth and few flowers. Seeds will need to be sown under glass in early spring. Sow thinly on top of a peat-based growing medium in pots or boxes. Prick off the seedlings into boxes, harden off and plant out in early summer. Spacing will depend on the cultivar you choose.

Take care
Remove faded flowers regularly.

Phlomis russeliana

▶ **Sunny location**
▶ **Well-drained ordinary soil**
▶ **Summer flowering**

This herbaceous perennial is closely related to the well-known 'Jerusalem Sage' (*Phlomis fruticosa*) and, in a border, creates a spectacular display with its tiers of whorled flowers. This handsome weed-smothering plant, or ground coverer, has large, rough, puckered, heart-shaped, felty, sage-like grey-green leaves. Among the foliage, stout flower spikes, 75-90cm (30-36in) high, carry whorls of soft rich yellow hooded flowers in early summer to midsummer. The attractive seedheads can be used successfully in flower arrangements, whether green or dried. Phlomis will grow in ordinary garden soil in an open, sunny location.

Propagation of this plant is by seed, cuttings or division, in spring or autumn.

Take care
Plant phlomis against a suitable background, such as a red-leaved Japanese maple.

Phlox drummondii 'Carnival'

(Annual phlox)
▶ **Sow in spring**
▶ **Ordinary well-drained soil**
▶ **Open, sunny site**

An easy-to-grow, half-hardy annual, *P. drummondii* will give a succession of colour throughout the summer. For a really bright display try the cultivar 'Carnival'; this mixture has pink, rose, salmon, scarlet, blue and violet flowers. The flowers are borne on stems 30cm (12in) high which carry light green lanceolate leaves. Blooms are produced in early summer as dense heads up to 10cm (4in) in diameter; each individual flower is rounded. These plants are ideally suited for low-growing areas of the garden, especially the rock garden.

In spring, sow seeds under glass in a temperature of 16°C (60°F). Use any good growing medium for sowing. Sow the seeds thinly and cover them lightly. Prick off the young seedlings, when large enough to handle, into boxes or trays. Harden off and plant out in flowering positions in early summer at 23cm (9in) intervals.

Take care
Dead-head to prolong flowering.

Above: Phlomis russeliana has whorls of rich yellow hooded flowers borne on stately spikes.

The basal leaves are heart-shaped and the seedheads are ideal for indoor decoration.

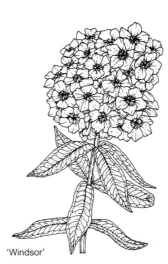

'Windsor'

Above: A sweetly scented dwarf mixture, Phlox drummondii 'Carnival' is summer flowering and includes a wide range of lovely colours with contrasting eyes.

Below: Physostegia virginiana 'Rose Bouquet' has spires of tubular pink-mauve flowers carried above the large, coarsely toothed leaves during late summer.

Phlox paniculata
(Fall phlox, Perennial phlox, Phlox, Summer perennial phlox)

▶ **Sun or light shade**
▶ **Light fertile soil**
▶ **Mid to late summer flowering**

These herbaceous perennials are some of the best border brighteners, with a wealth of musk-scented flowers borne in clustered heads. The times of the day to enjoy phlox to perfection are daybreak and sunset.

There is a wealth of varieties, in many colours: 'Windsor', clear carmine flowers with a magenta eye; 'Vintage Wine' with purple-red flowers; 'Prince of Orange' with orange-salmon flowers; 'White Admiral' with white flowers; and 'Mother of Pearl' with pink flowers. There are also some superb North American varieties with magnificent cylindrical trusses.

Phlox are best in light soils enriched with compost to retain moisture during dry summers. Phlox do not like chalk or clay soils. The only pest of major importance is eelworm. To avoid it, propagate plants from root cuttings in autumn or winter.

Take care
Do not let phlox dry out during summer.

Physostegia virginiana
(False dragonhead, Obedience, Obedient plant)

▶ **Sun or partial shade**
▶ **Any good fertile soil**
▶ **Late summer flowering**

This hardy herbaceous perennial is well named the obedient plant, because its flowers have hinged stalks and can be moved from side to side and remain as altered on their square stems. The long, narrow, dark green, glossy leaves are toothed and grow in four columns. The dull rose-pink flowers terminate the square tapering spikes, 45-105cm (18-42in) tall. They bloom from summer to autumn, until the frosts spoil their beauty. Physostegia has vigorous stoloniferous rootstocks that spread underground.

There are several good varieties: 'Rose Bouquet' has pinkish-mauve trumpet flowers; 'Summer Snow' is pure white and about 75cm (30in) high; and 'Vivid' bears rose-crimson flowers on stalks 30-45cm (12-18in) tall.

Propagate by division in spring or by root cuttings in winter.

Take care
Give this plant sufficient moisture during dry summer weather.

Pyrethrum roseum
(Chrysanthemum coccineum)
(Painted daisy, Persian insect flower, Pyrethrum)

▶ **Sunny location**
▶ **Good fertile soil**
▶ **Early summer flowering**

Many fine varieties of this herbaceous perennial have been introduced and named, both single and double forms. 'Eileen May Robinson', a large single pale rose-pink variety, has erect stout stems that are 80cm (32in) tall with flowers 7.5cm (3in) across. *P. roseum* 'Brenda' is also single, with Tyrian purple flowers 9.5cm (3.75in) across on erect 90cm (36in) stems. For a double form, choose the large-flowered pink 'Progression', 90cm (36in) tall or the pure white double 'Aphrodite', of perfect shape, 60-70cm (24-28in) high. All these are excellent as cut flowers.

Propagate pyrethrums by division in early autumn or early spring, doing this every second year. These plants will thrive in a fertile well-drained soil in an open, sunny position.

Take care
Support with twiggy peasticks, from early in the season.

Rudbeckia fulgida
(Rudbeckia speciosa, Rudbeckia newmanii)
(Coneflower)

▶ **Full sun**
▶ **Moist fertile soil**
▶ **Late summer and autumn flowering**

This herbaceous perennial has also been known as *R. speciosa* and *R. newmanii*, but, whatever one calls it, it is one of the most useful border and cut flowers in late summer and autumn. Erect 60cm (24in) stems rise from leafy clumps, displaying several large golden-yellow, daisy-like flowers with short blackish-purple central discs or cones, hence the name coneflower. The narrow leaves are rather rough to handle. Other garden forms of *R. fulgida* are the free-flowering *R.f. deamii*, 90cm (36in) tall, and 'Goldsturm' which, above its bushy growth, has stems 60cm (24in) tall carrying chrome-yellow flowers with dark brown cones. Rudbeckias make good cut flowers and blend very well with *Aster amellus* 'King George'.

Propagate by dividing the plants in autumn or spring.

Take care
Do not let these dry out during the summer.

Above: The bright flowers of Rudbeckia fulgida 'Goldsturm' are superb for cutting from late summer. They never fail to create beacons of colour in a border.

Right: In warm moist surroundings, Schizostylis coccinea 'Major' will thrive in most types of soil and produce these stunning star-shaped flowers.

Salvia × superba
(Salvia virgata nemerosa)
(Long-branched sage)

▶ **Sun or partial shade**
▶ **Any good fertile soil**
▶ **Early summer to late autumn flowering**

For many years this herbaceous perennial was known as *Salvia virgata nemerosa*. Each erect 90cm (36in) stem carries branching spikes of violet-purple flowers with reddish-brown bracts (modified leaves). Today there are also dwarf varieties, such as 'Lubeca' with masses of violet-blue flowers, 75cm (30in) high and 'East Friesland', violet-purple and only 45cm (18in) tall. These salvias look well when planted on their own.

Salvias are both fully hardy and perennial. They will grow in any good fertile soil or on chalk but they dislike dry soils and should not be allowed to dry out. Some form of support should be given, such as peasticks pushed in around the plants to allow them to grow through. Propagate salvias by division in spring or autumn.

Take care
Support the tall varieties.

Schizostylis coccinea
(Crimson flag)

▶ **Full sun**
▶ **Any moist fertile soil**
▶ **Early autumn flowering**

This rhizomatous herbaceous perennial from South Africa grows freely in most soils. In South Africa, it grows near water and needs ample moisture to flower. It has long stems, 60-75cm (24-30in) or more and pretty, cup-shaped flowers open in a star-like fashion, not unlike small gladiolus flowers. *S. coccinea* has rich crimson blooms about 4cm (1.6in) across. The varieties 'Major' and 'Gigantea' are even brighter and larger. 'Mrs Hegarty' is pale pink and 'Sunrise' has large pink flowers. The flowering stems are excellent for cutting.

The rhizomatous roots need to be lifted, divided and replanted every few years to keep them thriving. A spring mulch of peat or well-rotted garden compost will help to retain moisture around the plants. Propagate by division in spring, always leaving four to six shoots on each portion.

Take care
Be sure to keep them moist.

bove: Salvia × superba is a hardy nd adaptable plant that will thrive any soil. It produces abundant spikes of lovely violet-purple flowers over a long period from early summer.

Sedum spectabile 'Autumn Joy'

(Ice plant)
▶ **Full sun**
▶ **Well-drained soil**
▶ **Late summer/autumn flowering**

The name ice plant probably originated because this species has glaucous glistening foliage. The leaves are opposite or in threes and clasp stout erect stems 30-60cm (12-24in) high. Above these stems are borne flat, plate-like, unbranched flowers. *S. spectabile* has pale pink blooms. The varieties 'Carmen' and 'Meteor' are a deeper pink, and 'Brilliant' is a deep rose-pink. 'Autumn Joy' is at first pale rose, gradually changing to a beautiful salmon-pink. Later it turns a beautiful brown to give a pleasant winter display. The flat flower heads will be besieged by bees.

These border perennials can be grown with the minimum of attention. Propagate them by taking stem cuttings in midsummer and rooting in sandy soil in a cold frame, or by division in late summer or autumn.

Take care
Give these sedums room – about five plants to a square metre.

Solidago 'Goldenmosa'

(Aaron's rod, Golden rod)
▶ **Sun or partial shade**
▶ **Good ordinary soil**
▶ **Late summer flowering**

Golden rod, at one time, meant some small, yellow, one-sided sprays at the top of tall, stout, hairy stems. Today, there is a much larger section of these herbaceous perennials. The variety 'Goldenmosa' has pretty frothy flowers and miniature heads of the original golden rod, similar to mimosa. The rough hairy flower spikes are 75cm (30in) tall.

Two smaller varieties are the 45cm (18in) 'Cloth of Gold' with deep yellow flowers and 'Golden Thumb' with clear yellow flowers on 30cm (12in) stems, which produces neat little bushes ideal for the front of the border.

These vigorous plants will thrive in any good soil well supplied with nutrients. A sunny location or one in partial shade will suit them equally well. Propagate all varieties by division in spring.

Take care
Apply humus to taller varieties.

Far left: Sedum spectabile 'Autumn Joy' is easy to grow and spectacular in bloom with flowers that shade from pale rose to salmon-pink.

Left: Solidago 'Goldenmosa' is a superb variety with lovely frothy yellow flowers in late summer.

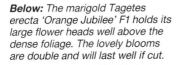

Below: The marigold Tagetes erecta 'Orange Jubilee' F1 holds its large flower heads well above the dense foliage. The lovely blooms are double and will last well if cut.

Tagetes erecta 'Orange Jubilee' F1

(Aztec marigold, African marigold, Big marigold)
► **Sow in spring**
► **Any soil**
► **Open and sunny site**

Marigolds are half-hardy annuals and are very reliable. The cultivar 'Orange Jubilee' is no exception. One of a strain of Jubilee types growing to 60cm (24in) tall, they are often referred to as 'hedge forms' because of the dense foliage. 'Orange Jubilee' is an F1 hybrid and, although seeds are relatively expensive, they are worth the extra cost because of the reliable uniformity of flower.

Carnation-shaped double blooms are produced on the almost erect stems of very sturdy plants. The blooms are light orange in colour and individual flowers can be 10cm (4in) in diameter. Foliage, kept below the flowers, is light green and deeply cut. All parts of the plant are very pungent. This cultivar can be used for nearly all purposes. The plant will look well formally planted with other complementary subjects. Plant out at 30cm (12in) apart.

Take care
Dead-head to prolong flowering.

Tigridia pavonia

(One-day lily, Shell flower, Tiger flower)
► **Sunny location**
► **Rich well-drained soil**
► **Plant 7.5-10cm (3-4in) deep**

These spectacular half-hardy cormous plants from Mexico and Peru can reach 60cm (24in) tall with long, sword-shaped, pleated leaves of mid-green. The flowers last only a day but each stem produces a succession of up to eight blooms in summer. These are up to 10cm (4in) wide and have three large petals with three small petals in between, surrounding a cup-shaped base. The larger petals are plain but the smaller ones are spotted in white, yellow or red, which gives them the common name of tiger flower.

Plant the corms in spring, 7.5-10cm (3-4in) deep in a rich well-drained soil and in a position where there is plenty of sun. Lift them in autumn and keep dry and frost-free until replanting time next spring. At this time, cormlets can be removed and grown separately, to reach flowering size in a couple of years. During winter, guard against mice eating the corms.

Take care
Keep moist in dry weather.

43

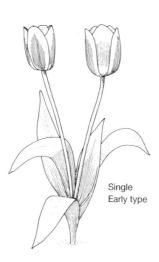

Single
Early type

Tradescantia virginiana 'Isis'

(Common spiderwort, Spiderwort, Widow's-tears)
▶ **Sun or partial shade**
▶ **Any good fertile soil**
▶ **Summer and autumn flowering**

The spiderworts are probably better known as house plants, but the hardy herbaceous perennials are much larger. *T. virginiana* has a number of varieties from which to choose. These perennials have smooth, almost glossy, curving strap-shaped leaves, ending in a cradle-like effect. A continuous display of flowers emerges throughout summer and autumn.

The variety 'Isis' has deep blue flowers and is 45cm (18in) high. The pure white 'Osprey' has three-petalled crested flowers. Another pure white of similar height is 'Innocence'. Two 50cm (20in) varieties are the carmine-purple 'Purewell Giant' and the rich velvety 'Purple Dome'.

Plant them in clumps, not singly. They are not effective on their own, but clumps make a splash of colour. Propagate them by division in spring or autumn.

Take care
Plant near the front of a border.

Tulipa

(Tulip)
▶ **Full sun**
▶ **Slightly chalky soil**
▶ **Plant about 15cm (6in) deep**

Tulips are bulbous plants that are so well-known that they do not need description. In addition to the many types created through selection and hybridization, there are other species that are also worth growing. These include *Tulipa clusiana* (the lady tulip), *T. kaufmanniana* (the water-lily tulip), *T. griegii* and *T. tarda*.

Man-made types include Single Early and Double Early forms, which can be planted in flower borders for spring flowering. Other forms include Mendels, Triumph, Darwins, Cottage, Rembrandt and Parrot types.

Plant the bulbs in late autumn, in slightly alkaline soil and full sunlight. Remove the flowers after they fade, but leave the stems and leaves attached to the bulb. If the space is needed for planting summer-flowering plants, dig up the bulbs – complete with stems and leaves – and replant them into a trench in a remote position.

Take care
Dead-head the plants to build up the bulbs for the following year.

Above: *Zinnia elegans 'Hobgoblin Mixed' is a bright mixture of medium-sized, weather-resistant double flowers.*

Left: *Tulipa 'Flaming Parrot' (Division 10) has large, exotic flowers which are heavily fringed and strikingly coloured.*

Below left: *Verbena × hybrida 'Florist Mixed' is a mixture with a spectrum of colours. Grow this dwarf verbena on the rock garden, border edges and in containers or window boxes.*

Below: *This mass of stunning, tall-growing and large-flowered tulips is the Darwin hybrid Tulipa 'Golden Apeldoorn' (Division 5).*

Verbena × hybrida 'Florist Mixed'

(Garden verbena, Verbena, Vervain)
▶ **Sow in early spring**
▶ **Any fertile soil**
▶ **Sunny position**

This half-hardy perennial is invariably grown as a half-hardy annual. The variety 'Florist Mixed' provides a diverse colour range. The stems, 23cm (9in) in height, tend to spread and make a mat. The rainbow shades of the flowers are produced above the foliage, which is dark green – this gives a jewel-like effect. This perennial is very useful as a front plant for window boxes, containers or flower beds and borders.

Sow seeds in pots or boxes in early spring under glass. Keep at a temperature of 16°C (60°F). Use any good growing medium. Prick off the young seedlings, as soon as they are ready, into boxes or trays. Harden off and plant out into flowering positions in early summer. Those for containers and window boxes can be planted out slightly earlier as long as they are in sheltered positions. Spacing should be 23cm (9in) apart.

Take care
Water freely in very dry weather.

Zinnia elegans 'Hobgoblin Mixed'

(Common zinnia, Youth and Old Age, Zinnia)
▶ **Sow in spring**
▶ **Ordinary well-drained soil**
▶ **Sunny position**

The 'Hobgoblin' mixture of this half-hardy annual has a range of colour in shades of red, pink, yellow and gold.

Zinnias make good bushy compact plants. The stems are about 25cm (10in) long and branched. The leaves are ovate, pointed and light green. Both stems and leaves are covered with stiff hairs. These plants are ideal for borders and beds in a bright, sunny situation.

As a tender half-hardy annual, this plant will need to be raised from seed under glass in spring. Sow seeds in any good growing medium that is free-draining. Keep at a temperature of 16°C (60°F). Prick out seedlings into individual peat pots; this will avoid handling the stems at a later date, which can be damaging. Grow on in the usual way and harden off at the end of spring. Plant out carefully in early summer, 23cm (9in) apart.

Take care
Avoid overwatering at any stage.

INDEX OF COMMON NAMES